How to DEAL WITH PEOPLE WHO —

DRIVE YOU ABSOLUTELY NUTS

— A Life Guide —

How to DEAL WITH PEOPLE WHO —

DRIVE YOU ABSOLUTELY NUTS

— A Life Guide —

Created by

DR. SUZANNE GELB, PhD, JD

FIRST EDITION

All rights reserved. This book or any portion thereof may not be reproduced or used in any manner whatsoever without the express written permission of the publisher except for the use of brief quotations in a book review.

Copyright © 2019 Dr. Suzanne J. Gelb, PhD, JD

Manufactured in the United States of America.

ISBN-13: 978-1-950764-10-5
ISBN-10: 1-950764-10-9

www.DrSuzanneGelb.com

PRAISE FOR... THE LIFE GUIDES

I wrote this life guide on how to deal with people who drive you nuts... without losing your cool, as well as 10 other life guides on various topics, to help readers successfully navigate some of life's trickiest challenges.

Each Life Guide includes educational information sourced from my three+ decades of coaching and counseling in the field of emotional wellness.

What Readers Are Saying

Praise

"Thank you, thank you, thank you.

Finally, I understand why kept losing it with my kids. Not cool!

Now I know how to keep a lid on things. I've read a lot of anger management books — nothing comes close to this guide. You rock!."

—Belinda

"I've tried so many things hoping to figure out why certain people rub me the wrong way.

Your guide gave me so many answers.

Finally! I'm so glad I found you and this Life Guide."

—Rick

"Dr. Gelb's Life Guide on People Who Drive You Nuts should be on everyone's bookshelf who ever got angry at someone else — even once!

Such simple wisdom, carefully explained.

My relationship with my husband is much calmer now, and the kids keep saying, "Mom, is something wrong?" That's because they're not used to the house being so quiet!"

—Karen

"Your guidebooks are gems."

—Alexandra Franzen, Published Author, Writing Teacher

CONTENTS

Disclaimer.   xiii

INTRODUCTION

Change How You Manage Your Emotions, Change Your Relationships.   1

WHAT'S INSIDE AND HOW TO USE THIS GUIDE   5

PART 1

"Why Am I SO Angry?!" Three Reasons Why It Feels Like That *%^*%$! Person Is Driving You Nuts.   6

PART 2

Why It's Important To Learn How To Deal With People Who Drive You Nuts… Instead of Just Avoiding Them or "Grinning and Bearing It."   24

PART 3

How To Release Negative Anger — Safely and Effectively. (A Three-Step Process.)   35

PART 4

Managing Anger in Your Everyday Life. (Five "Real World" Scenarios and Solutions You Can Try.)   52

A FEW FINAL WORDS

Becoming Calmer and Happier. 64

MORE TIPS, MORE TOOLS

FAQs About Dealing With Annoying People and Situations. 66

WHAT'S NEXT?

Resources… to Keep Learning and Growing. 88

ABOUT THE AUTHOR 99

OTHER BOOKS BY THE AUTHOR 100

INDEX 102

DISCLAIMER

This book is a tool that can help you to learn how to constructively deal with people (and situations) that drive you absolutely nuts.

This book contains educational exercises and tips drawn from my career in the field of emotional wellness with over 30 years of experience. This book is for informational purposes only, and is not intended to diagnose or treat any illness, nor is it a substitute for professional or psychological advice, diagnosis, or treatment. Always consult a qualified health care professional before engaging in any new, self-help resource (such as this one) and with questions you may have about your health and wellbeing.

Any case material that may be alluded to in this book, including in articles, or in interviews [see Resources section] does not constitute guarantees of similar outcomes for the reader. No results can be promised, since everyone's personal development path is unique. Names and details have been changed for privacy.

Links inside this book to external websites are for informational purposes only. Linking does not imply endorsement of or affiliation with that site, its content, or any product or service it may offer.

All link URLs in this book are current at the time of printing. Link URLs may fail at some point if the page has been deleted or moved. The author assumes no responsibility or liability for broken links.

This concludes the disclaimer portion of this book.

Thank you. Enjoy this Guide ... and enjoy your life.

INTRODUCTION

Change How You Manage Your Emotions, Change Your Relationships

Welcome to the Life Guide on How To Deal With People Who Drive You Absolutely NUTS.

It might be the way that he talks.

It might be the way that she behaves.

It might be something that you can't quite pin down…

— **The way that they "look" at you**?

— That **"cocky" tone** in their voice?

— **A sense that they are misleading you**?

or that

— **A sense that their intentions are in the wrong place**?

For all of these reasons and so many more (which we'll discuss, at length!) …

Some people just make you feel soooo angry!

Except, that's not exactly true.

No one has the power to "make" you feel angry.

No one has the power to "make" you feel anything, actually.

That's a myth.

Sure, people can do things that are annoying, even infuriating, but in every instance,

YOU get to choose how you are going to manage your emotions.

YOU get to choose how you are going to respond…

With:

— Explosive anger,

or with:

— Patience and compassion.

Making that kind of choice might feel **"hard"** or even **"impossible,"** with certain oh-so-annoying people. But…

having the right tools can make all the difference.

This Life Guide will give you the tools to deal with people who drive you nuts… **without:**

— **blowing up**,

— **screaming**,

— **yelling**,

or

doing something else that you might regret.

However:

Reading this Life Guide isn't enough.

For the tips and tools in this Life Guide to be effective, you need to be willing to practice them in your everyday life.

After all:

You can't...

— **buy** an instrument,

— **never** practice it,

and

— **expect** to become a masterful musician!

Practice is what creates progress.

So, get ready to:

- **learn**
- **reflect**

and

- **practice, practice, practice.**

Consistent, diligent practice of the tools, as they are outlined in this Life Guide, can mean that:

A calmer, happier, more peaceful future awaits.

Let's begin!

What's Inside and How To Use This Guide

Inside this Life Guide, you'll find a series of lessons to help you learn how to **deal with people** (and situations) who **drive you nuts** — so that you can **keep your cool...** no matter what is going on around you.

Each lesson includes fill-in-the-blank worksheets.

The lessons are designed to support you to not only:

— **Understand** and **manage** your emotions more effectively,

but also to:

— **Connect with** your **true self** (which is wise, calm and loving),

so that you can be equipped to:

— **Use your anger constructively** without blowing up, yelling, or doing something else you may regret.

The Contents page of this Life Guide gave you a peek at what's ahead.

PART I

"Why Am I SO Angry?!" Three Reasons Why It Feels Like That *%^*%$! Person Is Driving You Nuts.

"This person drives me nuts! I can't stand being around them!"

Over the past 3+ decades, I've heard lots of clients express frustration about:

— *"that ONE person"*

or

— *"certain people who shall not be named."*

Often, prior to working with me, my clients feel **"justified"** in their anger.

"He is such an inconsiderate jerk!

I have every right to be angry!"

Other times, my clients feel **unclear** about the origin of their anger.

"She hasn't done anything that bad...

Why am I having such strong feelings about this?"

I've found that, generally speaking, there are **three reason**s why certain people can trigger such intense emotions.

In this section of this Life Guide, I'll describe each of those reasons.

So,

The next time it feels like someone is driving you nuts, you might want to stop and ask yourself:

"Which of these three reasons might apply to me, right now, in this scenario?"

"Why am I SO angry?"

REASON NUMBER 1

It's conceivable that…

— the person you're angry at reminds you of:

- **someone else**,

or of:
- **a past situation**, where you felt **a similar kind of anger**.

Examples:

- Your **controlling boss** reminds you of your **controlling mother**, who chose all of your clothes for you and never allowed you to express yourself in the way that you desired.

- Your **colleague** is **very critical** of the work that you do… **just like your dad**, who constantly **found fault** with everything you did.

The circumstances and the people involved might be different, but the feelings are similar.

It's possible that you might have **swallowed** (in psychological terms, "suppressed") some (or all) of the anger that you felt during those previous situations.

That could be why your anger feels so **intense** right now.

Why?

Because:

— not only are you experiencing anger about the **current situation**,

but conceivably…

— **repressed anger** from the past has also **bubbled up to the surface**.

This can feel like a double, triple or quadruple wave of anger. Anger from the present AND the past, swirling into one big storm!

And the next thing you know…

— you're having an **inappropriate outburst**,

or

— some other **exaggerated** response…**way out of proportion** to what the current situation warrants.

"Why am I SO angry?"

REASON NUMBER 2:

It's conceivable that…

— you have **an expectation that is not being met.**

Examples:

— You **expect your assistant to** do what she says she's going to do,

but then….

— **she doesn't.**

— You **expect your husband to** make plans to celebrate your anniversary without being reminded,

but then…

— **he doesn't.**

When we expect people to behave in a certain way, and then they don't conform to our expectations, it's not uncommon to feel a rush of anger.

If they keep violating our expectations, it's conceivable that:

— our **anger** will **keep building and building,**

and eventually...

— **erupt in an unhealthy way**...

UNLESS

— **we know how to manage it, effectively**.

So, how can you handle your anger when someone doesn't meet your expectations?

First, you'll need to:

- **release your anger safely** so you can **restore inner calm**.

    (more on how to do this in Part Three of this Life Guide).

Then, you'll need to:

- **acknowledge that** (oops!) you were **holding onto an expectation**.

Example:

"I had a specific expectation about how this would go.

I forgot, momentarily, that everyone — including myself — has free choice and free will."

And then, you'll need to:

- **forgive yourself** for creating an **expectation**.

Let it go.

Now, **instead of** thinking,

"This person is driving me nuts! I can't stand them!"

Your thoughts can take on **a calmer tone**.

Instead, you might think:

"I don't appreciate what this person is doing.

This is not something I support.

To the extent possible, I intend to do something productive about it."

And then, from that **calmer place**, you can:

- **make a wise choice** about how to proceed.

Examples:

— **discontinue** the relationship,

— **reiterate** what you require and won't compromise about

and / or

— **enforce** consequences...

In other words...

you can make a choice to do whatever your good judgment calls for you to do.

The goal, of course, is:

— not to impose your expectations on others to begin with.

Instead,

— you can **honor yourself** by, to the extent possible, associating with people who share **similar standards**...

Meaning:

People who are "**on the same page.**"

This can **open the door to amazing possibilities.**

"Why am I SO angry?"

REASON NUMBER 3:

It's conceivable that:

— **You're (really) angry at yourself**.

Examples:

- Your boss is piling extra work onto your plate, and you're furious...

    but deep down,

    you're mostly angry at yourself, because...

    you agreed to work overtime when you knew that was not what you wanted to do.

- Your child is throwing a tantrum (again!) and you're feeling angry ...

    but deep down, you're mostly angry at yourself, because...

    you haven't enforced the household rules, and now, you've got a little tyrant on your hands who doesn't know how to behave.

Self-directed anger can be like a red traffic light — signaling you to stop making certain choices, now.

Examples:

— Stop saying "Yes" to your boss, when you mean "No."

— Stop giving into your child, when you need to be firm.

If you don't start making different (better) choices, it's likely that people will continue to do things that you don't want them to do.

But…

THEY'RE not really the problem.

YOU need to make different (better choices).

This may sound harsh, but it's actually a very empowering fact.

Because…

it means that you are in the driver's seat.

Reflect and respond.

Think about someone who makes you feel:

- angry,

- bitter,

- annoyed,

even

- infuriated.

Which of these three reasons do you think might be causing this to happen?

Or…

Do you think it's **a mixture of a couple of reasons**?

But what if it's… NOT one of those three reasons?

That's entirely possible, too.

Read on for some illumination about what might be happening with you…

"I know someone who doesn't really drive me 'nuts'.

My feelings aren't that intense.

It's more like…

I just don't like them.

Why does that happen?"

Sometimes, we simply "don't like" certain people or situations.

Not because we're holding onto unresolved, pent-up emotions.

Simply because... we have certain preferences.

And that's OK!

Examples:

It's OK to prefer:

— the music of Mozart over heavy metal.

It's OK to prefer:

—grilled chicken sandwiches over tuna salad.

It's OK to have preferences about the kinds of people that you invite into — and keep in — your life.

Checklist:

If you can **look within** and **honestly say to yourself**:

"I don't particularly like this person, but…

- *This person **doesn't remind me of** someone else in my past, who I didn't like.*

[check! it's not Reason Number 1.]

- *I'm not feeling really really angry because they are not meeting my expectations.*

[check! it's not Reason Number 2.]

- *I'm not angry at myself.*

[check! it's not Reason Number 3.]

- *This person just isn't my cup of tea.*

It's a preference.

That's all."

Then that is:

— **perfectly healthy**

and

— **reasonable**.

Everyone is entitled to have their preferences.

Including you!

"What if I think it's just a 'preference'... but I'm not sure?

Is there a process that can help me to know for sure?"

Yes.

There is an **emotional check-in** that you can do to **get clearer about** whether:

— your "preference" **really is a "preference"**...

and not:

— a form of **suppressed anger.**

Here's an example to illustrate how this "check-in" works.

Imagine you're getting into a taxi and the driver is blasting loud music that you don't like.

A **reasonable, healthy response** would be to say to the driver:

"Excuse me.

Could you please turn down your music?

I'd appreciate it."

If the driver **ignores** you or doesn't want to comply, **a reasonable, healthy response would be** to think to yourself:

"Jeez, that's seriously rude.

Oh well. He's obviously unwilling to accommodate me, so I'll just relax and let it go.

We'll be arriving in five minutes, anyway.

It's not that big of a deal."

This kind of response...

— **not happy**,

but

— **willing to let it go...**

reflects **positive submission**.

Positive submission is a term used by some psychologists to refer to a particular type of **"letting go."**

It essentially means that:

you change what you can, while accepting and letting go of things that are outside of your control.

You're not

— "giving up"…

Instead you're

— "lightening up."

Instead of harboring anger, you're making peace with life's limitations and making the best of the moment.

If your initial irritation with the cab driver is **truly rooted** in a **preference**, nothing else, you would be able to:

- **shift into positive submission**

    with **relative ease**.

"This isn't my preferred situation,

but I can let it go."

If your initial irritation with the cab driver was **NOT rooted** in a preference, but rather, **some other reason** (like suppressed anger because the driver reminds you of your inconsiderate father...)

- you would **NOT be able to shift** into positive submission

    very easily.

Instead, you'd probably:

— get **furious**,

— **obsessively re-play** the cab incident in your mind for the rest of the day,

or

— **lash out** by screaming at the driver

or by,

leaving a **"poison-soaked" customer review** on the cab website.

TO RECAP:

If you suspect that your dislike for a particular person is based on a **preference**, nothing more, here's what you can try next:

See if you can shift into a state of positive submission.

Is it **easy** to do?

Great.

Then you're probably right:

— it's a **preference**!

If it's **not** easy to do,

— then your **irritation might be rooted in something**... else.

And if that's the case?

It's important to learn how to:

- **deal with those feelings**

rather than

- **ignore or avoid them.**

Why is that true?

I'll explain in Part 2 of this Life Guide.

PART 2

Why It's Important To Learn How To Deal With People Who Drive You Nuts... Instead of Just Avoiding Them or "Grinning and Bearing It."

Clients often say to me something along these lines:

"Why do I have to learn how to deal with people who annoy the heck out of me?

Isn't that a form of self-abuse? Putting myself in those situations that trigger such unhappy feelings?

Wouldn't it be easier just to:

- *cut those kinds of people out of my life...*

or

  - *avoid them, forever?*

I'd be so much calmer and happier!"

To address that question, I'll use a metaphor.

Imagine that you're trying to stop overeating and lose weight... and **cheesecake** is one of the foods that you turn to when you're **seeking comfort** from food

(like when you're feeling negative emotions, such as intense fear or anger).

Imagine that you're having one of those ***"I'm hungry for comfort"*** moments.

So...

— you open the fridge, and gaze upon a slice of cheesecake...

and,

— you feel out of control.

Before you know it, you're scarfing down the cheesecake — and that makes you **really disappointed with yourself**.

Why?

Because...

You're overeating and **sabotaging your efforts at success**. It's the worst!

When it's over, you solemnly swear to **never** even look at a slice of cheesecake again, and you say to yourself:

"I'll never buy it again...

I'll never order it again...

I just can't 'trust' myself around cheesecake!

I'm going to avoid it!"

Except,

the next day at work…

wouldn't you know it!…

Someone has baked a cheesecake and thoughtfully chosen to share it with the office.

It's sitting right by your desk.

DARN IT!

What are you going to do?

- Leave work and go home?

- Change your commuting route so that you never drive past a bakery?

- Move to a nation where cheesecake doesn't exist?

You see how silly this line of reasoning is.

You can't avoid cheesecake forever, and even if somehow you managed that, here's what could very well happen:

— some other food would just rise up to claim its place.

Because:

Avoiding the issue isn't the same as resolving the issue.

The **pent-up emotions** that are causing you to overindulge on the cheesecake **are still there**.

Why?

Because:

— you haven't yet released them.

Until you do that, cheesecake — or its equivalent — is likely to always have power over you.

It's exactly the same with **people who drive you nuts**.

You can't avoid these kinds of people, forever, unless...

you choose to live like a hermit in the woods.

It's far more empowering to learn how to:

— deal with people who irritate you, (safely and calmly)

rather than:

— just trying to avoid them.

When you learn how to do this,

you can become like:

— a monk who can meditate in the midst of an earthquake.

When you learn how to do this,

Nothing can rattle you.

No one can send you into a rage-spiral.

Nothing can pull you away from your natural state, which is Love.

And THAT is real power.

Write ... and reflect.

When you encounter people who drive you nuts, what is (or, are) your go-to response(s)?

— **Pretend** it's not happening?

— **Deny** your feelings?

— **Leave** the situation?

— Try to **avoid** that person forever?

— **Explode** with anger?

and / or...

— **Something else**?

Write as down many of your "go-to responses" that you can think of.

Try not to:

— **over-think**

or

— **edit** your responses.

Just **express** your thoughts, **freely**, as they pop into your mind.

Fill in the blanks:

When I encounter people who drive me nuts, one of my go-to responses is

_____

_____

_____

_____

When I encounter people who drive me nuts, one of my go-to responses is

_____

_____

_____

_____

When I encounter people who drive me nuts, one of my go-to responses is

_____

_____

_____

_____

Write ... and visualize.

Now, imagine, and / or visualize, that your True Self — your wisest, calmest, most loving self — is in the driver's seat.

Imagine and / or **visualize** that:

Your True Self is making the calls and running the show.

Now, **think** about:

— the last time (or a recent time) when you had an encounter with someone who annoyed you.

Now, **reflect** on this next question:

If your True Self was deciding how to handle things, what would your True Self choose to do?

Take your time to ponder this question...

Take a few relaxing breaths

— inhale deeply...

— exhale gently...

Enjoy this moment to listen to your inner wisdom ...

And when you feel ready, it's time to write down your answers.

Write ... and affirm.

Now, write and then affirm, what your True Self — your wisest, calmest, most loving self — would do the next time you have an encounter with someone who annoys you.

But…

Before you do this next exercise, keep in mind that:

Positive affirmations don't always work.

"What?!" you might say.

"Then why would I do this next exercise?"

Because…

Positive affirmations can be very effective, as long as they are created and expressed with total honesty and self-respect, and they're not just something that temporarily boosts our mood.

That's why I wrote this next article, that was published online in Tiny Buddha. If you want to, take a look at the article, or, if you feel ready, start the next exercise.

Why Positive Affirmations Don't Always Work (and What Does).

https://tinybuddha.com/blog/why-positive-affirmations-dont-always-work-and-what-does/

Fill in the blanks.

Then **affirm** what you wrote — in your mind or out loud.

If I have an encounter an annoying person, I handle things by

_____

_____

_____

_____

If I have an encounter an annoying person, I handle things by

_____

_____

_____

_____

If I have an encounter an annoying person, I handle things by

_____

_____

_____

_____

Congrats!

You've just taken an important step by tuning up your mindset with these positive affirmations.

But don't be all that surprised if, after a few days, you hit an **"emotional speed-bump."**

It's not uncommon for people to run into this, if they do affirmations, but don't resolve the strong feelings that caused them to be "over the top annoyed" at someone.

Why does this happen?

Why don't positive affirmations always last?

Because invariably in these situations, the emotions (e.g., angry feelings) are so intense that sooner or later the anger tends to override the affirmation — and essentially neutralize it.

Again, this is why it's so important to deal with the emotions, rather than ignore them.

How can these emotions be resolved?

I'll share a process in Part 3 of this Life Guide.

PART **3**

How to Release Negative Anger — Safely and Effectively (A three-step process.)

Think about the last time that you experienced something that really annoyed you.

— Maybe your child took money from your wallet without your permission.

Or

— Maybe a colleague at work kept talking to you and gossiping when you were trying to get your work done.

Or

— You ordered a salad in a restaurant with the dressing on the side. But when the waiter set your salad in front of you, it was drenched in dressing!

In that moment, you probably experienced what some psychologists call "**natural anger.**"

If "natural anger" could speak, it would calmly say something like,

"This is not OK with me. I want to do something about this."

The next logical step would be to:

— Take **appropriate action** to bring about a **positive change** — to rectify the situation **calmly** and **quickly**.

Natural (or positive) anger fuels us to make positive changes.

And so…

Natural anger is a very good thing!

Without it, we'd be **unmotivated** to:

- **improve**

or to
- **change** anything.

But…

When natural (positive) anger gets bottled up — like steam inside a pressure cooker — that's when it can turn into unnatural (negative) anger.

That's when we:

- **lose our cool**,

- **scream** at our kids,

- **rebuff** our colleague

or

- **curse** at a customer service representative.

It's important to learn how to release negative anger, appropriately — so that it doesn't become a force for destruction.

Here's one way to do it...

How to release negative anger — safely and effectively. A three-step process:

- **catharsis,**

- **correlation,**

- **rewrite the script.**

Have you seen what very little children do when they are:

— hungry,

— tired,

— afraid

or

— uncomfortable?

Little children express their feelings physically — by using their bodies.

They:

— cry,

— kick

or

— pound on a soft surface (like a crib)…

until they've **completely released all of the emotional energy** that needs to be released.

This is a very natural process for facilitating the release of their emotions.

And it's a process that you can mirror — albeit, in a more "grown-up" way — when you need to release emotional energy, too.

Right now, I will share a three-step process that has helped lots of people to **release their emotions** — rather than letting these emotions **get "stuck" or "bottled up" inside**, and then possibly fester and lead to self-loathing thoughts and behaviors.

STEP 1: Catharsis

Grab a pillow and a hand-towel.

Tie a knot in one end of the towel.

Situate yourself in a private space, where you'll be uninterrupted for a few moments.

It could be your study, even the bathroom if need be, or your garage.

Lock the door, if you can.

Then,

Focus your thoughts on the person and / or situation that's driving you nuts.

How do you feel?

— furious,

— frustrated,

— enraged,

— irritated…?

These are all versions of anger, and there are quite a few more.

To discharge this type of anger, **pound the pillow** with the **knotted end of the towel**.

While you're doing this, **verbalize how you're feeling**.

For example:

If you're angry at your spouse, you might direct your anger towards the pillow, as you pound it with the knotted towel, and say:

"I'm so mad that you don't honor my wishes! What's wrong with you?!"

Or,

Simply repeat:

"I'm so mad at you!

I'm so mad at you!

I'm so mad at you!"

Keep pounding the pillow and verbalizing how you feel.

As you keep doing this, **your words may change**, and **the focus of your anger might change** — perhaps to an earlier time when you felt mad at someone who didn't pay attention to your requests.

Don't :

- analyze what you're saying

or

- second-guess yourself.

Trust yourself.

Trust that…

— you're expressing exactly what you need to.

Trust that…

— this expression is being guided by your inner wisdom.

Trust that…

— you're not making this up.

Trust, also, that…

— you'll know when to stop.

Either because:

— you have a time limit

(you need to go and pick the kids up from school),

or

you'll just "know."

You'll feel that you've gotten to a point where you are complete or want to pause.

In my work with clients, I call this process :

- "The Pillow Pounding Technique,"

or

- "The Pillow Technique"

or "

- "The Process"...

depending whom I chatting with, and what term works best for them.

The terms are all synonymous.

In psychological terms, this process is called "**Catharsis**."

Once you feel complete with your Catharsis, at least for the moment, you can move on to Step 2 of our three-step process.

STEP 2: Correlation

The next step in the process is to correlate.

This means:

— To **connect the dots**, so to speak,

and,

— **Determine what is fueling your feelings**…

To find the root cause, if you can.

Next time you're feeling:

- **super angry**

or

- **annoyed** with someone,

you can ask yourself the following question:

"When have I felt this way before?"

Trust whatever age comes to mind.

— It might be 1 or 2 years old.

— It might be 10 or 15 years old.

Perhaps someone **said** something to you back then

or

Perhaps someone **did** something that conveyed to you that **what you wanted didn't matter**

(like your wishes weren't important.)

Invariably, if you keep asking yourself this question —

"When have I felt this way before?"...

you'll make some connection with something that occurred during the **first six years** of life.

This makes sense, since that's when **our basic attitudes about ourselves and life are formed**.

We're like a **sponge** during those early years, absorbing everything we see and learn about life... from our caregivers and our surroundings.

You will probably make:

— **some kind of connection**,

or have:

— **some memory** of something that contributed to how you're **feeling now**,

even though ...

— that was **a long time ago**.

With that knowledge in place, you're ready for **the next step** in this **emotional healing process**:

Rewriting the script

(or, again in psychological terms, as some psychologists might refer to it — **insight** and **behavior change**.)

One side note, though, before we move on:

Sometimes, when people ask

"When have I felt this way before?"... **nothing** comes to mind.

- **No** connections.
- **No** childhood memories.
- **Nothing**.

If that happens for you, that's totally OK.

An answer may pop into your mind a bit later —

but even if it doesn't,

it's still very healthy

and necessary to

discharge your negative anger, safely, by pounding a pillow, as outlined above in Step 1.

STEP 3: Rewrite the script

Hopefully, by now, you have some:

— **insight** into the circumstances that

— **angered you long ago**,

and that are

— **fueling** some of the **intense reactions** you're currently experiencing.

"Oh, I get it!

My father never paid much attention to my requests...

and my husband forgets and ignores my requests...

just like my dad did!

No wonder I feel so annoyed!"

Armed with these insights, you're ready to

— **"rewrite the script."**

In other words,

you are ready to:

change your thinking — which also changes your behavior.

Your rewrite might look something like this:

*"That was **then**, this is **now**.*

I'm no longer that young child *being hurt by my dad's inattentiveness, over and over.*

I can heal that wounded part of me*, with loving words, understanding and kindness.*

I can replace my dad's negative script *(the one that said that what I wanted didn't matter)* ***with a new, healthier message:***

That

my desires <u>do</u> matter...

And that

I deserve to have them fulfilled."

With this new script in place, **the next time your husband ignores your wishes**, your anger is likely to be:

— **in proportion** to the situation,

instead of:

— **totally out-of-proportion**.

Why?

Because **you won't be reliving angry feelings from the long-distant past**.

Those feelings will have been **resolved**.

You can **apply this three-step process**:

1. Catharsis
2. Correlation
3. Rewriting the Script

to any negative emotion you may be experiencing.

Any negative emotion that is:

- exaggerated,
- excessive,
- making you uneasy or uncomfortable

or

- just plain won't let up!

Can't go through the three-step process, right this second?

Buy yourself some time.

You may not always be able to retreat to a private space to safely address your anger, on the spot.

— You might be talking to your boss when you feel deeply enraged,

or

— driving your kid to soccer practice,

or

— in the check-out line at the supermarket.

Sometimes, you may have to "buy yourself some time" and put your feelings on a shelf, so to speak, until you can properly take care of them later.

You can say to yourself,

"I am having some strong emotions that I need to deal with, and I will do that as soon as I possibly can. But now is not the time."

"Buying some time" isn't the same as:

— **suppressing** your feelings,

or

— **pretending they don't exist**.

You <u>are</u> going to take care of your feelings, just not right at this moment.

Wondering if this three-step process is <u>really</u> necessary?

In short:

Yes.

And it's proven to be very effective with clients I've counseled, as well as in my research.

All of these techniques may seem a bit "**awkward**" at first — or seem like **an awful lot of work!** — but in time, and with practice, this three-step process is likely to become **very natural** and **automatic**.

You'll sense when you "need" it,

and

You'll guide yourself through it…

just like you:

— **feed yourself when you're hungry**,

or

— **sleep when you're tired**.

And of course, if you're not finding it that easy to get the process I've just outlined, to "work" for you, don't hesitate to **reach out to a qualified professional** for support.

You deserve to make this effort for yourself.

You're worth it!

PART **4**

Managing Anger in Your Everyday Life (Five "Real World" Scenarios and Solutions You Can Try.)

In the previous section, you learned a three-step process that can help you to release negative anger safely and effectively.

Of course, it's one thing to understand how to release anger "**in theory**" and it's another thing to understand **how to do it in your everyday life**.

In this section, I'll share a few "**real world" examples** of how these tools can be applied.

I hope each of these mini-stories are helpful to you.

SCENARIO 1

Someone at work is always slacking off.

They start late, take long lunches and leave early.

No one seems to care.

But it bothers you and makes your workload heavier, since you have to pick up this person's slack.

Today, you notice that this person is about to leave work even earlier than usual, **leaving you with even more work to do.**

You feel:

- irked,

- furious,

- resentful.

You might want to:

Scream and spew out a nasty, heated response.

But instead, try:

Discreetly taking a deep breath and setting your feelings aside until you can deal with them later, safely and in private.

Meanwhile try the old faithful "counting to 10" method

(it can buy you time to think before you speak, instead of angrily blurting something out in the heat of the moment).

Then...

if possible, speak to whoever was bothering you, privately.

Be:

- empathetic

and

- understanding,

but

- factual.

"I realize that you have a lot of demands on your time, but I'd really like to sit down with you and get your ideas on how we can distribute the work more evenly."

This assertive approach will hopefully:

— Open the door to having an **important** and **necessary** conversation with this person.

You'll be using your anger in a healthy way — to create positive change — instead of a destructive way.

SCENARIO 2

Your partner knows that you like to live in a clean, tidy, organized house ... but they seem to be experiencing chronic memory issues.

They leave:

— dirty laundry on the floor.

— wet towels everywhere.

— crumbs on the counters.

And they

— don't put the cap on the toothpaste!

Such disrespect! What the heck?!

You feel:

- furious,
- frustrated,
- painfully ignored.

You might want to: Scream and Shout,

"How many times do I have to tell you to...!!"

But instead, try:

Discreetly taking a deep breath and setting your feelings aside until you can deal with them later, safely and in private.

And try, in this moment, to:

Accept what "is."

This doesn't mean you're:

— giving up

or

— letting your partner walk all over you.

It means: acknowledging that:

— you've done everything you can to try to rectify the situation

You've:

— asked,

— pleaded,

— begged,

— reminded.

So now…

it's time to relax and stop the fight.

Tidy up...

Not because

— you're acting like their mother (or father),

but because

— **it's the way you want things to be.**

You're tidying up for YOU, not for them.

SCENARIO 3

Your child has a lousy attitude…

He talks back and won't listen or do what you say.

Nothing you try is working and you're at your wits end.

You're fantasizing about those blissful days before The Little Monster came into your life.

If you hear one... more... sassy comment...

arghh!

You feel:

- **frustrated**,
- **furious**,
- caught in a **power struggle**.

You might want to:

- scream,
- yell,
- blame,
- criticize.

But instead, try:

Discreetly taking a deep breath and setting your feelings aside until you can deal with them later, safely and in private.

Then pause and ask yourself,

"What's the best way to handle this situation?

As a responsible parent, what would be the best approach?"

Most likely, this will involve **positive discipline.**

This means:

— **Consistently implementing reasonable consequences for inappropriate behavior,**

instead of

— **letting things slide.**

SCENARIO 4

You ask your boss if you can discuss a problem with him.

He is sitting at his desk, reading a document.

Without looking up, he nods as if to say,

"Yes, go ahead."

You describe the problem, while he continues to read the document.

He then gives you a suggested solution, without making any eye contact, whatsoever.

You feel:

- furious,

- resentful.

You might want to:

Grab that document out of his hands and rip it up.

But instead, try:

Discreetly taking a deep breath and setting your feelings aside until you can deal with them later, safely and in private.

Then:

— **calmly** thank your boss for the suggestion.

Then, later, when you have a moment:

Try using the three-step process outlined in Part Three of this Life Guide to release your anger, safely.

Then:

Try to figure out why this particular scenario is "pushing your buttons" so intensely.

I once had a client who experienced a similar situation. He found that not getting direct attention from another adult — like his boss — reminded him of when he was a child, never getting undivided attention from his mother.

This insight helped him to see that:

The anger he was feeling about the current situation was more about the past than the present.

This, in turn, allowed him to:

Handle the present situation in an appropriate manner, without flaring up.

SCENARIO 5

There's a colleague, employee or friend who consistently disappoints you.

You feel like you're clearly expressing what you want and need, but **this person continues to fall short**.

— They're always late...

or

— flaking out...

or

— doing a lackluster job.

It's becoming a huge drain.

You feel:

- **extremely frustrated,**

- **Annoyed,**

- **irritated**

and

- **impatient.**

You might want to:

— Tell them off in the loudest, harshest terms

and / or

— "shake" (or "knock") some sense into them.

But instead, try:

Discreetly taking a deep breath and setting your feelings aside until you can deal with them later, safely and in private.

Remind yourself that:

You are in charge of your emotions.

You get to choose how to respond.

A FEW FINAL WORDS

Becoming Calmer and Happier.

When you learn how to reconnect with your True Self — your wisest, calmest, most loving self — this can transform **every moment**, and **every relationship,** in your life.

When your True Self is in the driver's seat — guiding your thoughts and actions — it means that:

You can use your anger constructively (say, to make a positive change)

rather than bottling it up so that it could become harmful to you, and to others.

Remember:

When you lose your cool, there's a reason why it's happening — and there are steps you can take to prevent it from happening again in the future.

You have learned several steps and tools right here in this Life Guide.

It will take practice, but the more you practice using these new tools in your everyday life, the more natural and automatic these processes can become.

You can do it.

Thank you for taking the time to learn how to manage your emotions more effectively.

Because of people like you —**people who are striving to change old patterns and replace them with healthier ones** — our world can become a calmer, happier place.

MORE TIPS, MORE TOOLS

FAQs About Dealing With Annoying People and Situations.

Now that you've read Part 1 through Part 4 of this Life Guide, you know more about about why "certain people" are soooo annoying — and how to handle these kinds of scenarios with grace. Here are even more tips and tools to continue your journey to deal with people who drive you absolutely nuts.

Read on for my answers[1] to some of the more typical questions I've been asked over the past 3+ decades as I've helped people learn to keep their cool — no matter what's going on around them.

---

[1] The questions and answers are summarized here, to maximize your learning experience.

Question No. 1 — So cocky and arrogant

Replacing Expectations With Observations

I have a dear friend whose very smart and artistic. When she offered to review some of my artwork (I'm painter) and give me constructive feedback, I welcomed that opportunity.

What I didn't anticipate though, was that when she gave me her feedback, she would be condescending and arrogant.

That's what happened. Even though some of her feedback was constructive, and even helpful, her cocky attitude made the whole experience very unpleasant.

After she was finished giving me her feedback, I felt like I had been put through the wringer... like I'd been in a boxing match where I sustained more than a few blows.

For the rest of that day, I was so mad. All kinds of angry thoughts were going through my mind, like:

"How dare she talk to me that way!"

"Who does she think she is!"

"She has no right to trample all over my artwork like she did!"

"What's wrong with her... what's her problem?"

"I don't ever want anything to do with her ever again!"

The problem is that I would like to continue receiving her feedback, but how do I not let her arrogance bother me?"

Response:

I'm all too familiar with the type of behavior you describe.

Often individuals who engage in this type of behavior have a heart of gold, and, deep down, they are some of the nicest people.

But they've built this outer veneer of arrogance and cockiness.

And it can drive some people, like yourself, absolutely nuts.

But then, as with yourself, there's a dilemma:

"I really don't want to end this relationship

But…

I can't deal with this person's personality.

So what do I do?

What can I do?"

Remember:

People have free choice.

This means that:

Although we might **expect** them **to behave in a certain way,**

(e.g., *"If you're going to give me feedback, I expect you to be respectful and polite as you do so."*)

They **may not choose to behave** in the way **we expect** them to.

If someone doesn't behave as we expected them to, this invariably triggers a reaction in us — we see red! We experience INSTANT ANGER.

The fix?

Let go of expectations.

Why?

Expectations can never be satisfied, all of the time.

Why?

There will be times when someone will choose to behave differently to how you expect them to behave.

— You may not agree with how that person chooses to behave…

and

— Their behavior may not always be in line with what you want,

or

— What you even believe is right.

You're entitled to your opinion and preferences.

But still...

Other people get to choose their own behavior.

That said, of course there are consequences (positive or negative) for choices that people make.

Some people have trouble wrapping their minds around this concept of people getting to behave as they choose (despite there being consequences).

As one person put it,

"How can I be OK with someone behaving in a way that I know is unacceptable?

Aren't I, then, lowering my standards of what is acceptable behavior?"

Keep in mind that:

It's not about:

— lowering your standards.

It's not about:

— compromising on your values.

It's about the difference between:

- **Hoping** that someone will behavior in a certain way,

verses

- **Expecting** that they behave in a certain way.

TO RECAP:

It's perfectly fine to hope that someone will behave in a certain manner.

But don't expect it.

When we expect someone to behave in a particular way, we're setting ourselves up to **instant anger.**

Why?

Because people have free choice.

And if someone chooses not to behave as we "expect" them to… you're living proof of what happens next:

Instant anger.

So…

When we

- **Replace expectations with observations**

  ("How interesting that she is so cocky and arrogant!")

then:

- **It can be so much easier to co-exist with someone else's behavior that we find unappealing,**

but where:

- **We still want to engage with them**

Because overall:

- **The positives of our experience with them outweigh the negatives.**

Question No. 2— So manipulative and demanding

Releasing Anger and Frustration, Safely

My coworker has a really annoying habit of always needing to be right, and to have the last word.

I've been paired up with her to work on a project that spans a nine-month timeframe — and it may end up taking longer.

We're two months into the project and I'm pulling my hair out! She's driving me nuts. She manipulates everything I say by telling me I said things that I didn't and no matter what I say, even if I know she thinks the same way, she'll counter it with something contrary... just to have the upper hand.

In a nutshell, if I say "black," she says "white"... and vice versa. My boss's temperament is similar temperament to hers, so I'm hesitant to talk to him about the situation.

Top that off with the fact that my boss is putting too much work on my plate - it's just not reasonable.

But I'm relatively new at this job, which is quite prestigious and sought-after in my profession, so it's like I'm at the point where I'm still paying my dues and earning respect. So I don't want to complain too loud and make the waves.

But between my boss and my coworker, I'm angry all the time. Even my wife says my personality is changing and she points out that I now have road rage, which I never used to have. What can I do to be able to put up with these people who infuriate me?

Response:

I applaud you asking this question because with what you're encountering — two people in your work environment who are infuriating to you... you're like:

— a ticking time-bomb that could explode at any time...

or

— a volcano on the verge of eruption.

This is compounded by the fact that you work closely with one of the people who infuriate you.

In addition,

— your relatively newly-manifested road rage suggests that your pent-up anger and frustration is at the point where you can no longer contain it.

[Note to readers: At this point in my response to this person, I provided an outline for the three step process for releasing negative anger, similar to the process that you read about in Step 3 of this Life Guide: "How To Release Negative Anger — Safely and Effectively. (A Three-Step Process.)"

I also shared some "real world" scenarios with this person, to walk him through how he could apply these tools to his daily life.

The scenarios, that I shared with him, were similar to the ones you read about in Part 4 of this Life Guide: Managing anger in your everyday life (Five "real world" scenarios and solutions you can try).]

You would be wise to release your anger safely and consistently, using this three-step process **on a daily basis** for a while.

This way, you are likely to:

— Avoid getting so backed-up emotionally

That when you interact with your coworker or your boss...

— You're at risk for erupting emotionally

And then...

— Saying things that you wish you hadn't ... but can't take back.

And worse yet,

— Unleashing your anger, aggressively, at a driver who irritates you (road rage.)

Regarding your boss, unfortunately, unreasonably demanding bosses are all too common.

So much so that I wrote an article about this challenging subject.

It's called, **How to Deal With Unreasonable Demands From Your Boss, and** was published on my online column, "Be Well At Work," in The Muse.

https://www.themuse.com/advice/how-to-deal-with-unreasonable-demands-from-your-boss

As you read through the article, you'll see that, again, I point out the importance of the:

Safe release of pent-up emotions so that:

- **You'll be better equipped to maintain calm composure**

(which will support productivity, whereas pent-up anger will not).

Think of your daily practice of releasing your anger safely like:

— **Going to the emotional gym, every day.**

Except with the emotional gym, it's

— **Super convenient** (right in your own home),

— **Quick** (5 - 10 mins per day, 1 - 2 x per day typically does it)

and it

— **Doesn't cost anything (it's free!)**

and, when the **emotional workouts** are done:

— **properly**

and

— **effectively.**

The results are:

— **rapid,**

— **powerful,**

— **inspiring**

and

— **impressive.**

So now that you have this **simple, user-friendly process** in your emotional toolbox, you can begin to:

— turn this **potential nightmare situation** at work

into a

— **meaningful challenge**

that can

— reap great benefits in terms of **emotional freedom**

as you demonstrate to yourself that:

"I am in charge of my emotions.

No one can 'make' me feel a certain way.

When I'm faced with irritating people and / or situations, it's up to me whether I:

- *react explosively
  (erupt)*

or

- *respond calmly
  (choice)*

No one can 'get under my skin' unless I permit it.

I can manage my anger.

I am managing my anger.

Anger (mine or other people's) is no longer my enemy.

Anger (mine or other people's) is now my teacher and my friend."

Question No. 3 — So passive and accommodating

Accepting the Consequences of our Choices

I've been married for 5 years. My wife is special and we get along great, except for one thing....

When it comes to her family, she always puts them first — even before our marriage!

If her father calls and wants her to do something, she'll drop whatever she's doing (even if she and I are having a special dinner together) and cater to him.

She's always been this way and it makes me so mad. I talk and talk and talk to her about this until I am blue in the face. I try to get through to her that:

"You have to grow up.

Our life is more important than pleasing your parents.

I didn't sign up for this, you know!"

It seems like she "hears" what I am saying... and she says she understands the point I'm making... but she still keeps behaving the same way.

I'm irritated a lot of the time because of this. Even just the mention of her family turns me off now and I can feel a knot of anger in my gut. How can I get through to her so she can see that she needs to put our marriage, and our relationship, first — before her family?"

Response:

It appears that:

You Are Experiencing the Consequences of Your Choices.

That doesn't mean that these consequences are necessarily pleasant or fun.

But it's important to recognize that that's the reality of what you're dealing with.

Specifically, in the description leading up to your question, you said:

"She's always been this way and it makes me so mad."

The fact that "she's always been this way," indicates that **you were aware of this behavior** trait of hers **before you married her**.

But — without pointing finger or passing blame — the fact is that **you chose to marry her, nonetheless**.

But now…

You're wanting to **change** something about your partner that you essentially agreed to **accept**, when you married her.

It's as if you're wanting to turn back the clock and undo a decision that you made years ago. But in reality, that's not possible.

Ask yourself:

"Am I being fair to my wife?

I married her, knowing full well that she is an overly doting daughter, and that her biological family comes first (i.e., she drops everything for them.)

But now...

I'm expecting my wife to be different than the person that I agreed to marry, because I've now decided that I don't want to live with certain behaviors of hers that I didn't previously object to."

Hopefully, after having run through this script, you can see that while it would be wonderful if your wife would change her behavior (if that would be in her best interests to do so)...

The change that you're seeking must start with you.

It begins with you:

Safely, and effectively, releasing your anger and frustration about:

- Your wife's behavior

And possibly even about:

- The fact that you agreed to marry her years ago, fully aware of this behavior.

Only after doing this, can you be in a frame of mind to be able to:

- Make peace with the fact that you made a choice years ago, accept the consequence of the choice you made years ago

    (i.e., you married your wife, knowing she was overly doting on her biological family.)

This may seem like a harsh reality and reasoning that is quite blunt — but again, it's simply a factual picture of "what is."

[*Note to reader:*

At this point in my response to this questions, I outlined a three-step process for releasing negative anger, safely and effectively.

The process that I outlined was similar to the process that you read about, earlier, in Part 3 of this Life Guide.

I then laid out the three questions below, for the purpose of self-reflection.]

Ask yourself?

"What are my options from this point forward?

Do I:

• Continue to stay angry?

Or, do I:

- ***Process my feelings using the three step process?***

And then

- ***Accept the consequences of a choice I made years ago?"***

Positive ending:

Fortunately, this person chose to use the three-step process to manage his anger in a healthy way.

It took practice, but in the end, he became more accepting of his wife's behavior, even though, he still wishes she'd shift her priorities and make their marriage (not her family) number one!

That said, **he is no longer trying to get her to change** her behavior.

Instead, **he has changed** how he deals with her behavior.

- ***He no longer reacts, angrily, to her behavior.***

Instead,

- ***He has learned how to co-exist with her behavior.***

Now that's success!

Question No. 4 — So irresponsible and annoying

Identifying the Lessons to Learn and Positive Steps To Take

My two co-workers are always slacking on the job when they can get away with it.

But they're really good at pretending to be "on top of things" when my manager or boss stops by the cubicles where they work.

I see what they do behind the scenes... they're like two teenagers trying to see what they can get away with. And they get away with a lot!

And then they have the nerve to complain that they don't get paid enough. Can you believe that!

They really bother me. I'm always so annoyed when I'm around them... I feel like I'm turning into a person who is always angry and I don't like feeling this way.

But it's so unfair... and even though I don't want to quit my job, I don't know how I can go to work and not be annoyed by these two coworkers because I see them all the time.

On top of that, I really can't say anything to anyone about this because I think it would be interpreted as me being "sour grapes" and "ratting on coworkers." I'm thinking of quitting my job because of this but I'm wondering, "Is that my only way out?"

Response:

It seems that you have concluded that there isn't any constructive action or positive steps that you can take to try to rectify the situation that you feel is unfair.

You might then want to take a look at positive steps that you can take to release and resolve the negative emotions that you are feeling when you're at work.

This way, although…

- **We CAN'T necessarily change what's happening around us,**

- **We CAN take steps to positively change how we feel about what's happening around us.**

That's where our power resides.

You might want to start by asking yourself the next three questions.

Then, **fill-in-the-blanks** with your answers.

— Try not to overthink or edit what you write.

— Just write whatever comes to mind.

— Allow your feelings to pour out of you, freely.

1. *I'm so annoyed and irritated. When have I felt this angry before?*

_____

_____

_____

_____

2. *What is the lesson that I need to learn, in this situation?*

_____

_____

_____

_____

3. *What is one positive step that I can take?*

_____

_____

_____

_____

To understand more about how answers to these three questions can be helpful when it comes to:

• Restoring inner calm when we're in the presence of annoying people

take a look at the article that I wrote on this topic.

It's called:

Why "Certain People" Make Us Feel Completely Insane and How to Reclaim Our "Zen"
— Published online in Positively Positive

http://www.positivelypositive.com/2015/02/05/why-certain-people-make-us-feel-completely-insane-and-how-to-reclaim-our-zen/

After reading the article, you can **fill-in the blanks** to the three questions for a second time, if you'd like.

This can a be good start to beginning to gain some insight into:

— **Why** your "emotional buttons" are being pushed,

and

— **How** you can begin to respond differently when you're in the presence of people like your coworkers, who drive you nuts!

WHAT'S NEXT?

Resources... To Keep Learning and Growing

This Life Guide is "technically" complete, but I wanted to give you some **more resources on dealing with situations that can trigger strong emotions (e.g., anger, frustration, irritation, etc), stress and self-care** (because when you take care of yourself, you're more likely to feel good about yourself and be able to handle challenges such as annoying people) ... in case you want to continue the learning and the growing with me.

Here are some of my favorites — articles I've authored,[2] books I've written, and inspiring insights that I shared when I was interviewed by a reporter from the Weekend Today Show, to savor at your leisure.

Enjoy!

---

[2] Except where otherwise noted, all articles referenced in this section were published online.

Dealing with situations that can trigger strong emotions (e.g., anger, frustration, irritation, etc.)

How to Deal With a Co-worker You Don't Like—But Everyone Else Is Obsessed With
— Published in Dr. Gelb's column, "Be Well At Work," on The Muse.

https://www.themuse.com/advice/how-to-deal-with-a-coworker-you-dont-likebut-everyone-else-is-obsessed-with?ref=carousel-slide-0

Why "Certain People" Make Us Feel Completely Insane And How To Reclaim Our "Zen."
— Published on Positively Positive.

https://bit.ly/2HOCdAg

How to Deal With Unreasonable Demands From Your Boss
— Published in Dr. Gelb's column, "Be Well At Work," on The Muse.

https://www.themuse.com/advice/how-to-deal-with-unreasonable-demands-from-your-boss

Throwing a Tantrum? Having a Meltdown? Paralyzed With Fear? Your Heart Might Be Frozen In Time
— Published on Positively Positive.

http://www.positivelypositive.com/2015/05/16/throwing-a-tantrum-having-a-meltdown-paralyzed-with-fear-your-heart-might-be-frozen-in-time/

How to Do a Great Job Even When You Don't Like Your Job
— Published in Dr. Gelb's column, "Be Well At Work," on The Muse.

https://www.themuse.com/advice/how-to-do-a-great-job-even-when-you-dont-like-your-job

Career Envy: What To Do When A Friend Gets The Job You Wanted
— Published in Dr. Gelb's column, "Be Well At Work," on The Muse.

https://www.themuse.com/advice/career-envy-what-to-do-when-a-friend-gets-the-job-you-wanted

Taking Care of an Elderly Parent -- and Not Loving It? How to Turn Resentment Into Patience and Joy
— Published on The Huffington Post.

http://www.huffingtonpost.com/dr-suzanne-gelb/caregiving_b_5260566.html

"Still Mad at Your Parents? How to Forgive and Move On, Once and for All"
— Published on Positively Positive.

http://www.positivelypositive.com/2014/08/07/still-mad-at-your-parents-how-to-forgive-and-move-on-once-and-for-all/

3 Ways to Get What You Need From Terrible Communicators
— Published in Dr. Gelb's column, "Be Well At Work," on The Muse.

https://www.themuse.com/advice/3-ways-to-get-what-you-need-from-terrible-communicators?ref=autocomplete

How To Do an Effective Timeout. [3 tips for parents whose kids just won't cooperate...]
— Published on The Huffington Post.

http://www.huffingtonpost.com/dr-suzanne-gelb/how-to-do-an-effective-timeout_b_6472216.html

Why Positive Affirmations Don't Always Work (And What Does)
— Published on Tiny Buddha.

http://tinybuddha.com/blog/why-positive-affirmations-dont-always-work-and-what-does/

Why I Still Believe People Can Change
— Published on Positively Positive.

http://www.positivelypositive.com/2014/12/15/why-i-still-believe-that-people-can-change/

Dealing with stress

Stressed Out at Work? How to Cope -- Without Turning to Food or Booze
— Published on The Huffington Post.

https://www.huffpost.com/entry/stressed-out-at-work-how_n_6711034

If You Want to Make Tomorrow Less Stressful—Start Tonight
— Published in Dr. Gelb's column, "Be Well At Work, on The Muse.

https://www.themuse.com/advice/if-you-want-to-make-tomorrow-less-stressfulstart-tonight

Don't Feel Like Exercising? 3 Steps To Get You Off The Couch
— Published in Dr. Gelb's column, "All Grown Up," on Psychology Today.

https://www.psychologytoday.com/blog/all-grown/201505/don-t-feel-exercising-3-steps-get-you-the-couch

How to Find Work That You Love When You're Stuck in a Job That You Hate (A Life Guide)
— by created Dr. Gelb

https://amzn.to/2YmrFO2

How to Succeed Everywhere: 10 Tips for Balance at Work, Home, in Relationships
— Written by Shelby Marra, published online on NBC's Today.

https://www.today.com/health/how-become-high-achieving-woman-work-your-relationship-parent-t33071

Side note: As my colleague, friend, and gifted writing teacher, Alex Franzen said: *"THIS IS AMAZING! Being interviewed by a reporter from NBC's Today Show? Uh, that's the big leagues!"*
Yes, that's what happened. Shelby Marra with NBC's Today Show in New York, requested an interview with me so that she could write this article featuring me, for TODAY.com's Successful Women series.

How Successful People Do More in 24 Hours Than the Rest of Us Do in a Week
— Published on Newsweek; also published on The Muse.

https://www.newsweek.com/career/how-successful-people-do-more-24-hours-rest-us-do-week

Side note: The Muse is an online platform that attracts more than 75 million people each year, to help them be at the top of their game at work.

I'm honored to have received the praise below, from Adrian Granzella Larssen, Editor-in-Chief, in response to an article that I wrote for The Muse:

"Wow! This is fantastic stuff. You're clearly incredible at what you do, and I'm so thrilled to share your advice with our audience!"

Spring Cleaning For Your Life [part 1 / 3]. A checklists for parents to create a more peaceful, productive home dynamic.
— Published in Dr. Gelb's column, "All Grown Up," on Psychology Today.

https://www.psychologytoday.com/blog/all-grown/201603/spring-cleaning-your-life-part-1-3

What to Do If a Child Won't Respond to Rules or Consequences
— Published in Dr. Gelb's column, "All Grown Up," on Psychology Today.

https://www.psychologytoday.com/intl/blog/all-grown/201808/what-do-if-child-wont-respond-rules-or-consequences

Can You Imagine… Your Kids Being Cooperative?
— Published in Dr. Gelb's column, "All Grown Up," on Psychology Today.

https://www.psychologytoday.com/blog/all-grown/201602/can-you-imagine-your-kids-being-cooperative

8 Simple Truths About Raising Happy, Successful Kids
— Published in Dr. Gelb's column, "All Grown Up," on Psychology Today.

https://www.psychologytoday.com/blog/all-grown/201508/8-simple-truths-about-raising-happy-successful-kids

Three Lessons You Must Teach Your Kids. (The sooner the better. But it's never too late)
— Published in Dr. Gelb's column, "All Grown Up," on Psychology Today.

https://www.psychologytoday.com/blog/all-grown/201503/parents-three-lessons-you-must-teach-your-kids

"Just Believe." How I Learned To Trust In The Universe, Even When All Hope Seemed Lost
— Published in Positively Positive.

http://www.positivelypositive.com/2015/03/26/just-believe-how-i-learned-to-trust-in-the-universe-even-when-all-hope-seemed-lost/

Feeling Phone-verwhelmed? 5 Tips To Help You Create A Healthier, Happier Relationship With Your Smartphone
— Published in Dr. Gelb's column, "All Grown Up," on Psychology Today.

https://www.psychologytoday.com/blog/all-grown/201508/feeling-phone-verwhelmed

Self-Care

You Are The Best Investment You'll Ever Make
— Published in Dr. Gelb's column, "All Grown Up" on Psychology Today.

https://www.psychologytoday.com/blog/all-grown/201511/you-are-the-best-investment-youll-ever-make

6 Self-Sabotaging Habits You Need To Drop Right Now
— Published on Mind Body Green.

https://www.mindbodygreen.com/0-14014/6-selfsabotaging-habits-you-need-to-drop-right-now.html

The Greatest Cheerleader One Can Have — Lives Within: How to Stay Strong When Not Everyone is Cheering For Our Success
— Published in Dr. Gelb's column, "All Grown Up" on Psychology Today.

https://www.psychologytoday.com/us/blog/all-grown/201902/the-greatest-cheerleader-person-can-have-lives-within

The Love Tune-Up: How to Amp Up the Love That's Naturally Inside You to Enjoy Happy, Healthy Relationships — A 14-Day Course That Can Change Your Life

https://amzn.to/2XQ7190

Welcome Home: Release Addictions and Return to Love

https://amzn.to/2vwXmIa

5 Ways to Stop Yourself from Eating When You're not Hungry
— Published on Psych Central.

http://psychcentral.com/blog/archives/2014/10/30/5-ways-to-stop-yourself-from-eating-when-youre-not-hungry/

Learning To Feed My Hungry Heart: My Journey From Bingeing To Wholeness
— Published in Dr. Gelb's column, "All Grown Up" on Psychology Today.

https://www.psychologytoday.com/intl/blog/all-grown/201904/learning-feed-my-hungry-heart

You Want Couple's Counseling But Your Partner Does Not. Are You Doomed?
— Published on Dr. Gelb's column, "All Grown Up" on Psychology Today.

https://www.psychologytoday.com/blog/all-grown/201504/you-want-couple-s-counseling-your-partner-does-not

Why People Resist Seeking Therapy
— Published on Dr. Gelb's column, "All Grown Up" on Psychology Today.

https://www.psychologytoday.com/blog/all-grown/201510/why-people-resist-seeking-therapy

**"What Actually Happens During A Therapy Session?"...
And 6 other common questions about psychotherapy**
— Published on Dr. Gelb's column, "All Grown Up" on Psychology Today.

https://www.psychologytoday.com/blog/all-grown/201512/what-actually-happens-during-therapy-session

ABOUT THE AUTHOR

Dr. Suzanne Gelb, Ph.D., J.D. is a psychologist, life coach, television commentator and author. For 3+ decades, she has helped people learn how to keep their cool — no matter what's going on around them, using tools like the ones in this book.

Dr. Gelb's inspiring insights on emotional wellness have been featured on more than 200 radio programs, 260 TV interviews, and online on Time, Newsweek, Forbes, Psychology Today, The Huffington Post, NBC's Today, and many more.

As a contributing writer to the The Muse (an online platform that attracts more than 75 million people each year,) Dr. Gelb has written articles on how to handle stressful situations, including, How to Deal With Unreasonable Demands From Your Boss, and How to Deal With a Co-worker You Don't Like—But Everyone Else Is Obsessed With. Her powerful articles, Why "Certain People" Make Us Feel Completely Insane And How To Reclaim Our "Zen" and Throwing a Tantrum? Having a Meltdown? Paralyzed With Fear? Your Heart Might Be Frozen In Time, were published on Positively Positive.

Dr. Gelb believes that it is never too late to become the person — you want to be. Strong. Confident. Calm. Creative. Free of all of the burdens that have held you back — no matter what happened in the past.

To learn more, visit www.DrSuzanneGelb.com.

OTHER BOOKS BY THE AUTHOR

It Starts With You – How to Raise Happy, Successful Children by Becoming the Best Role-Model You Can Possibly Be. A Guidebook For Parents.

How to Get Your Kids to Cooperate and Help Them Become the Best Grown-Ups They Can Be. (A Life Guide.)

Helping Your Teen Make Healthy Choices About Dating and Sex. (A Life Guide.)

How to Get Ready to Be a Parent and Be the Best Mom or Dad You Can Possibly Be. (A Life Guide.)

How to Forgive the One Who Hurt You Most. (A Life Guide.)

Aging With Grace, Strength and Self-Love. (A Life Guide.)

How to Navigate Being Single and Savor Your Dating Adventure. (A Life Guide.)

The Love Tune-Up: How to Amp Up the Love That's Naturally Inside You to Enjoy Happy, Healthy Relationships.

How to Rekindle That Spark and Create the Relationship and Sex Life That You Want. (A Life Guide.)

How to Find Work That You Love When You're Stuck in a Job That You Hate. (A Life Guide.)

How to Reach Your Ideal Weight Through Kindness, Not Craziness. (A Life Guide.)

Welcome Home: Release Addictions and Return to Love.

How to Care for Yourself When You're a Caregiver for Somebody Else. (A Life Guide.)

Real Men Don't Vacuum. And Other Misguided Myths That Cause Conflict in Relationships.

INDEX[3]

A

accept what "is", 56
anger from the present and the past, 9
appropriate action, 36
avoiding the issue, 27

B

basic attitudes, 45
becoming calmer and happier, 64
behavior change, 46
"buy yourself some time", 49, 50

C

calm composure, 76
catharsis, 38, 40, 43, 49
change old patterns, 65
connect with your true self, 5
consequences of our / your choices, 70, 79, 80
controlling boss / mother, 8
correlation, 38, 44, 49
"counting to 10", 53

D

diligent practice, 4

E

"emotional buttons", 87
emotional check-in, 19
emotional freedom, 77
emotional gym, 76
"emotional speed-bump", 34
emotional toolbox, 77
exaggerated response, 9
expectations, 10, 11, 13, 18, 67, 69, 72
explosive anger, 2

F

forgive yourself, 11

H

honor yourself, 13
how to release negative anger, 35, 37, 38, 52, 74

---

[3] The page numbers in this index refer to the printed version of this book.

I

inappropriate outburst, 9
inner wisdom, 31, 42
insight, 46, 47, 61, 87
instant anger, 69, 71
intense reactions, 47

M

managing (my) anger, 52, 74, 78
my desires <u>do</u> matter, 48

N

natural (positive) anger, 36, 37
negative anger, 35, 37, 38, 46, 52, 74, 82
negative emotions, 25, 49

O

other people get to choose, 70

P

patience and compassion, 3
pent-up anger, 74, 76
pent-up emotions, 17, 27, 76
positive affirmations, 32, 34
positive submission, 20, 21, 22
pound the pillow, 40, 46

practice is what creates progress, 4
preferences, 17, 19, 70
"pushing your buttons", 61

R

"real world" scenarios, 52, 74
reconnect with your True Self, 64
release emotional energy, 39
release negative anger, 35, 37, 38, 52, 74
release your anger safely, 11, 52, 61, 75, 76
replace expectations with observations, 72
resolving the issue, 27
restore inner calm, 11
rewrite / rewriting the script, 38, 46, 47, 49

S

scenarios, 52, 66, 74
self-care, 88, 96
self-directed anger, 15,
solutions you can try, 52, 74
someone doesn't meet your expectations, 11
stress, 88, 92
support productivity, 76
suppressed anger, 8, 19, 21

T

"The Pillow Technique", 43
"The Process", 43, 44
three-step process, 35, 38, 39, 43, 49, 50, 51, 52, 61, 74, 75, 83
tools to deal with people who drive you nuts, 3, 66
trigger intense / strong emotions, 7, 88, 89
True Self, 31, 32, 64
trust yourself, 41

U

use your anger constructively, 5, 64

V

visualize, 31

W

we have certain preferences, 17
why am I SO angry?, 6, 8, 10, 14

Y

you get to choose, 2, 63
your True Self, 5, 31, 32, 64

www.ingramcontent.com/pod-product-compliance
Lightning Source LLC
Chambersburg PA
CBHW020143130526
44591CB00030B/194